Praise for
I LOVE MY PEOPLE

"Kim Singleton has penned a lyrical love letter to the world, lauding her people and leading joyful readers on a historical and current cultural journey as she pays homage to our ancestors, pioneers, and contemporaries. Her well-constructed lines evoke smiles of recognition; knowing nods recall and reflect the spirit and achievement that embody each singular name hailed from multiple genres—Martin, Toni, Michael, Ruby, Prince, and Serena, just to name a few. Selected images of historical references are added love notes. Encounters with our most familiar as well as lesser-known icons of Black excellence compel us to dig deeper and join in knowing, celebrating, and loving *our* people!"

— **Ambassador Alice M. Dear (RET)**, US executive director, African Development Bank (1994–2000)

"I love *I Love My People*: this poem is a reminder of our varied stories, our flavor, and our joy. Singleton invites us to celebrate the Black journey and experience with light and adoration."

— **Kandace L. Harris**, PhD, media scholar, higher ed administrator, and international president of the Howard University Alumni Association

"*I Love My People* feels like a lingering hug to Black culture in the form of a poem. It is an embrace that you want to come back to again and again because it's so soothing. Poet and author Kim Singleton has created a masterpiece—simple yet profound and all-encompassing. It's encyclopedic in the way it takes you on a historical journey. The phrase 'I love my people' reminds you of traditional call-and-response participation, like what happens in the Black church. Everytime you come to the 'chorus,' you feel like you're joining the congregation, saying in unison, 'I love my people,' with pride and gratitude. It gets louder and louder the more you read—until it soars to the heavens."

— **Kevin Harry**, publisher/photographer, *KHZines*

"*I Love My People* can easily be a classic poem that many will recite for years to come. It is a personal reboot of the good things in my life. As a stage and film producer, I look forward to seeing this piece performed with the enthusiasm and pride in which it was written. Kim Singleton has successfully affirmed the love affair we all have for our people. I join her in the mantra, 'I love my people!'"

— **Tony Wilkes**, founder, Phoenix Ensemble, Inc.

I Love My People

I LOVE MY PEOPLE

Cover images:
© Getty Images; White wood board by Katsumi Murouchi.
Photos from Kim Singleton and Wikimedia Commons 2022
Design: 1517 Media

Print ISBN: 978-1-5064-8671-0
eBook ISBN: 978-1-5064-8672-7
Printed in China

I LOVE MY PEOPLE

KIM SINGLETON

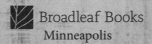

Broadleaf Books
Minneapolis

Creative names,
Saggy pants,
Soul train lines,
That wobble dance.

Fish fries, collard greens,
Urban slang,
Dudes named Pookie,
That dozens game.

I LOVE MY PEOPLE

Old men on corners
Talking trash,
Tell stories of old,
Of times long passed.

Jokes and cat calls
I can't escape,
But they keep watchful eyes
When I come home late.

I LOVE MY PEOPLE

Young boys on subways
Dance for change,
Doing it for survival,
Not flash or fame.

They flip and twist
With precision and skill,
And oh, so grateful
For that dollar bill.

I love
my people

I love my people

Micro braids, box braids,
Locs, and cornrows,
Finger waves, twist-outs,
Knots, and afros.

All types of textures
For all types of styles,
From 1 to 4c,
We're so versatile.

Designs for our hair
Go back centuries,
Reflecting our culture
And identity.

I love my people

Hip-hop, rap,
And R&B,
Godfather of Soul
Begging, "Please, please, please!"

Maxwell, Lenny Kravitz,
And my main man Prince,
Even Lil Wayne
Not making a lick of sense.

I love my people

Jimi, Michael,
Isaac, and Ray,
Changed musical landscapes
White imitators claimed.

Nina Simone
Voice deep and rich,
"My name is Peaches!"
Ooooo . . . I just love her pitch!

There's Ronnie, Bobby,
Ricky, and Mike,
From NWA to
Gladys Knight.

I love my people

Let's not forget
Our chocolate treats,
Like Denzel, Sidney,
And OG Billy Dee.

They fill the screens
With power and strength,
Qualities that all
Our Black men represent.

I LOVE
MY PEOPLE

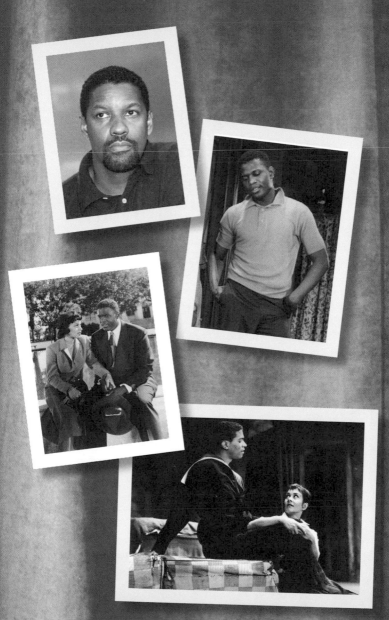

Our leading ladies
Have beauty and soul,
Indomitable spirit
Through meekest of roles.

Ruby, Eartha, Cicely,
To name a few,
My cinematic queens,
I bow to you.

I LOVE
MY PEOPLE

We were told that our bodies
Weren't built for this art,
Rhythmic movement we mastered,
Flowing straight from the heart.

Misty's ballet
Is perfect in form,
With Alvin's *Revelations*,
A classic was born.

I love my people

With Morrison, Baldwin,
Hurston, and Hughes,
Sharing intimate details
Of back home blues.

They also wrote stories
On equity, activism, and race,
Carving their prose forever
In America's literary space.

I love my people

Octavia Butler
My favorite of all,
In my thirst for sci-fi,
She answered the call.

Futuristic stories
Her imagination unleashed,
No other comes close,
May she rest in peace.

I LOVE MY PEOPLE

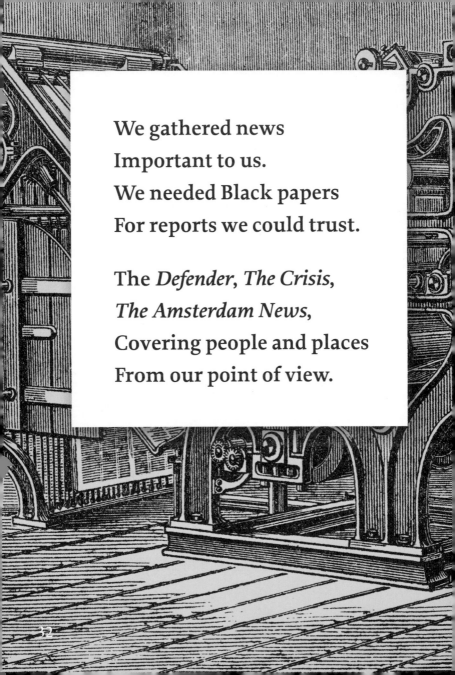

We gathered news
Important to us.
We needed Black papers
For reports we could trust.

The *Defender*, *The Crisis*,
The Amsterdam News,
Covering people and places
From our point of view.

THE CRISIS

THE CHILDRENS NUMBER
CRISIS
OCTOBER
1914

LIBER

33

Russwurm and Cornish
Were there from the start,
Publishing our stories
And new frontiers to chart.

In 1827,
Freedom's Journal was born.
Black content, Black operated,
Black staff, Black owned!

I love my people

Ebony, Jet, and Essence,
Beauty out front on the rack,
Showing once you go Black,
You can never go back.

First Black model
On the cover of Vogue
Was Beverly Johnson,
Radiant, regal, and bold.

Told it would never happen
She proved them wrong.
Paved the way for others
Including Naomi, Tyra, and Iman.

I love my people

We explored all continents
With an adventurous flair,
Inspiring future travelers
To discover and share.

There was Matthew Henson,
First on the North Pole.
Arctic exploration
Was his ultimate goal.

I love my people

Bessie Coleman soared
In international skies.
First Black woman pilot
Encouraged others to fly.

We conquered the Troposphere.
Oh, but we were not done.
The first Black woman in space,
Dr. Mae Carol Jemison.

I love my people

Neil deGrasse Tyson,
Astrophysicist.
His enthusiasm for science,
I can't resist.

Though big budget movies
Have plenty of clout,
Get your science facts wrong,
He will still call you out.

I LOVE MY PEOPLE

Solomon Harper, Sarah Boone,
And Elijah McCoy,
Black inventors made devices
That all could employ.

The oil drip cup, ironing board,
Hot curlers for your hair,
Refrigerated trucks, traffic lights,
And even the folding chair.

We have conceived and created
On technology's behalf,
Including a technique for eye surgery
By Dr. Patricia E. Bath.

I LOVE MY PEOPLE

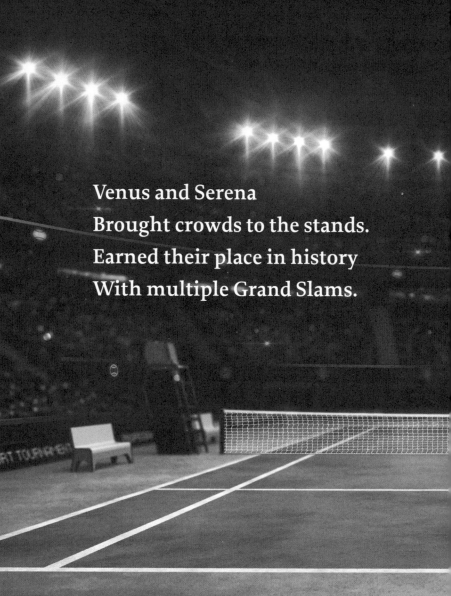

Venus and Serena
Brought crowds to the stands.
Earned their place in history
With multiple Grand Slams.

Bringing strength and speed,
We excel in all sports.
We are also game changers
Like Tommie Smith and John Carlos.

With gold and bronze medals
Obtained with all pride,
Raised their fists in the air
For Black Power worldwide.

From the field sidelines,
Kaepernick took a knee
To bring the attention
To police brutality.

I love my people

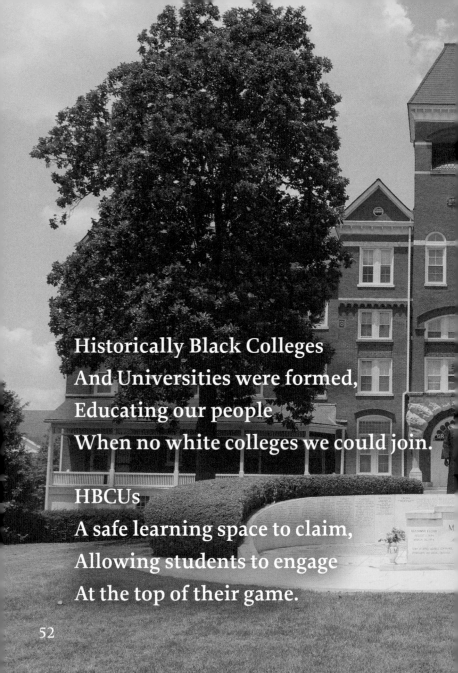

Historically Black Colleges
And Universities were formed,
Educating our people
When no white colleges we could join.

HBCUs
A safe learning space to claim,
Allowing students to engage
At the top of their game.

53

Producing doctors, lawyers,
Scientists, and priests,
Any profession out there
We've accomplished those feats.

Morehouse, Spelman,
Hampton, and Fam U,
Fisk and Lincoln
Also a part of that crew.

I went to Howard
And no matter where I go,
If I wear my Howard sweater
I'll hear "HU—You Know!"

I love my people

Black Greek Lettered Organizations,
Known as Divine Nine,
Provide fellowship and service
For a lifetime.

Starting with fraternities
In order of their year,
Amplifying brotherhood,
Which they hold dear.

Alpha Phi Alpha Fraternity,
Kappa Alpha Psi,
Next to be founded was
Omega Psi Phi.

Then Phi Beta Sigma,
And next on the list
Iota Phi Theta
Joined these altruists.

Alpha Kappa Alpha,
First Black sorority,
Then Delta Sigma Theta
Joined the D9 Tree.

Zeta Phi Beta and
Sigma Gamma Rho,
For more than a century
They've continued to grow.

I LOVE MY PEOPLE

The Tuskegee Airmen,
Skilled, dauntless, and staunch,
Came to the rescue
When World War II launched.

Aerial combat
Was their specialty,
Helped the US and allies
To true victory.

Though steadfast and brave
Up to the last day,
Still had no equality
When home in the States.

The Tuskegee Airmen,
Or Red Tails, they cry!
Their service to this country
Cannot be denied.

I love my people

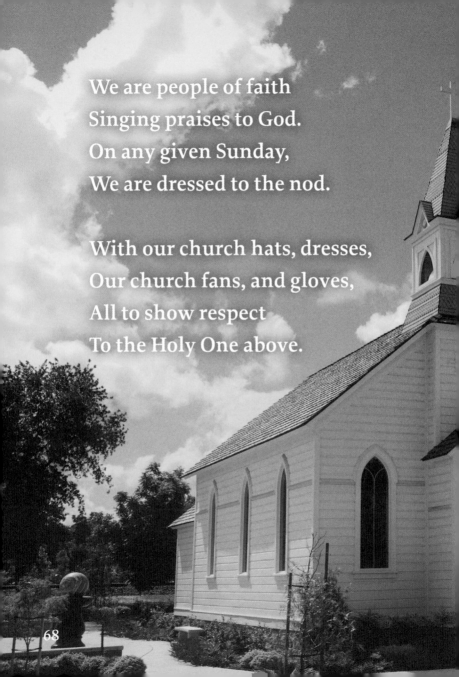

We are people of faith
Singing praises to God.
On any given Sunday,
We are dressed to the nod.

With our church hats, dresses,
Our church fans, and gloves,
All to show respect
To the Holy One above.

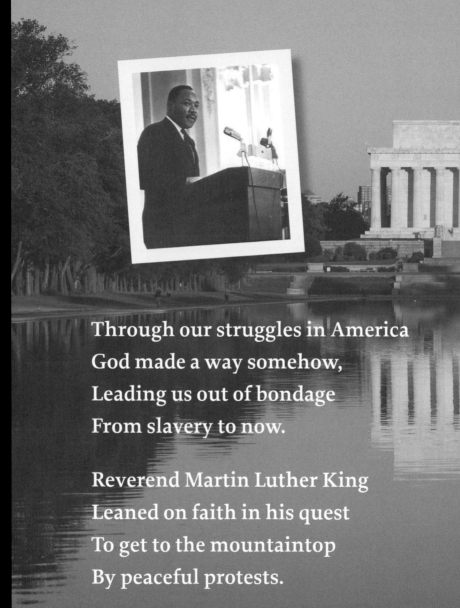

Through our struggles in America
God made a way somehow,
Leading us out of bondage
From slavery to now.

Reverend Martin Luther King
Leaned on faith in his quest
To get to the mountaintop
By peaceful protests.

I love my people

Ketanji Brown Jackson
Had more experience
Than all the other judges
That sat on that bench.

She was questioned and badgered
As if credentials didn't count.
Madam Supreme Court Justice,
Your perseverance won out!

I LOVE MY PEOPLE

There are all my peeps
Who fought for the cause,
They endured abuse,
Helped change the laws.

There's Thurgood,
Frederick Douglass,
My girl Fannie Lou,
Ida B, and Malcolm,
Oh, I love them too.

I love my people

75

There's Garvey, Du Bois,
And the relentless Daisy Bates.
There's the 44th President
Of the United States!

Shirley Chisholm,
Stacey Abrams,
John Lewis,
Represent!
There's Kamala Harris,
Madam Vice President!

Enduring injustices
That changed our lives,
By emerging even stronger
Like the Central Park, no,
the EXONERATED Five.

Some didn't make it,
They paid with death.
Their sacrifices
We'll never forget.

Hands up, don't shoot!
I can't breathe!
Until there is true justice,
This is our reprise!

I love my people

COLORED
WAITING ROOM

PRIVATE PROPERTY
NO PARKING
Driving through or Turning Around

BINGO
TONITE!

Good
Housekeeping

True Story

HITLER'S
LOVE LIFE
REVEALED

AITH BALDWIN'S
HAWAII

There are so many others,
Too many to name
From the corners of obscurity
To the highest of fame.

Kidnapped to this country
On ships in chains
Buried by Jim Crow,
Racism, lynchings, and pain.

Still, we rose
To the greatest of heights.
We will continue to rise
Never giving up the fight!

I LOVE MY PEOPLE

I love m

g people

Acknowledgments

My father, William Clarence Singleton II, was my original, unconditional, and ultimate supporter. His spirit is always with me.

The Singleton family is my constant source of inspiration. Thank you William III, Marc, Nichole, Carla, William IV, Cameron, Tyrell, Cydnei, Czarina, Harry Croxton III, and Aunt Geraldine Enright Finch. Most of all, thank you to our matriarch, Dr. D. Kim Singleton, who keeps everything and everyone together.

Encouragement and support from my second set of parents, Joseph and Angeloyd Fenrick, have been invaluable throughout my life.

The unconditional love from my friends, who are more like sisters and brothers, continues to keep me strong. Thank you Latisher Gaines, Jenyne Raines, Glenn Gilliam, Thelma Ramsey Bryant, Donna Johns, Joyce Stovall, Brenda Ross-Dulan, Brelinda Snoddy, Tanya Crossley, Alisa Drayton, April Patton, Erika Stroble,

June Townes, Cookie McCloud, Tony Wilkes, and Lawrence Winslow.

Thank you to my many circles of friends and colleagues, who have enriched my life more than you will ever know. My Central Senior High School crew, Howard University Bison crew, Abyssinian Baptist Church family, HBCU friends, and BGLO Divine Nine brothers and sisters are in my heart.

The journey with my beloved Alpha Kappa Alpha Sorority, Incorporated® has been one of supreme service and sisterhood. Thank you to Alpha Chapter, for starting it all; the Tenaciously Entwined 29, for choosing me; the Portentous Twist of 46, for being by my side; and the Tau Omega Chapter, for providing me a home.

Thanks to my first poetry instructor Jacqueline Johnson, for helping me find my voice, and all others who supported and loved me along the way. I love you.

Love and gratitude to my editor at Broadleaf Books, Adrienne Ingrum, for recognizing my work, setting me on this path, and sharing my work with a broader audience.

As always, sending praises to the One above, who was looking out for me when I wasn't looking out for myself.

Kim Singleton

Photo Credits

Page 55. Female Scientist Working in the Laboratory, Using a Microscope. Photo credit: sanjeri.

Page 55. Priest Performing Online in the Church. Photo credit: SeventyFour.

Page 55. Lawyer in a Courtroom. Photo credit: RichLegg.

Page 58. Locust Walk with Students in Fall, University of Pennsylvania. Photo credit: Jon Lovette.

Page 59. African Man Sitting inside a Library Alone Doing Research. Photo credit: Marco VDM.

Page 66. World War Two – Fallen Solider and American Flag Background. Photo credit: Keith Bishop.

Page 67. Tuskegee Airmen of the 332nd Fighter Group Flying near the Alps in Their P-51 Mustangs. Photo credit: Kurt Miller/Stocktrek Images.

Page 68. Old White Church. Photo credit: gchutka

Page 69. Lancaster Bomber aircraft. Photo credit: Sean Gladwell.

Page 70. Sunlight, Lincoln Memorial, Washington, DC, America. Photo credit: Joe Daniel Price.

Page 71. Praying Hands With Bible. Photo Credit: Christian Chan

Page 72. Judge Gavel. Continuous Line Drawing. By Natalie.

Page 73. Supreme Court Guardian of Law. Photo Credit: Perry Spring

Page 74. United States Capitol. Day. Flag. Photo credit: Andrey Denisyuk.

Page 75. Portrait of Fredrick Douglass. Photo credit: wynnter

Page 78. Freedom – Chains That Transform Into Birds – Charge Concept. Photo Source: RomoloTavani

Page 80. Fist Gesture One Line Art. Continuous Line Drawing of Hand Strength. By Drypsiak.

Page 84. People United against Racism – Anti-racism Protest. Photo credit: LeoPatrizi.

Wikimedia images and other photos used with permission:

Page 7. Two Youth with Baggy Jeans. Photo credit: William C. Singleton III.

Page 11. Breakdancing. Photo source: Wikimedia Commons/Raphael Xavier Williams (2005).

Page 17. James Brown Live in Hamburg, Germany (1973). Photo source: Wikimedia Commons/ Heinrich Klaffts.

Page 17. Prince Concert at Madison Square Garden in NYC (2011). Photo courtesy of Kimberly Singleton.

Page 17. Lil Wayne in Biloxi, MS (2015). Photo source: Wikimedia Commons/Megan Elice Meadows.

Page 19. Nina Simone in Bretagne, France (1982). Photo source: Wikimedia Commons/ Roland Godefroy.

Page 19. Ronnie Devoe, Bobby Brown, Ricky Bell, Michael Bivins of Singing Group New Edition at Sister Circle Live (2018). Photo source: Wikimedia Commons/Sister Circle Live.

Page 21. Denzel Washington (2000). Photo source: Wikimedia Commons/S. Jaud (de: Benutzer-Falkenauge).

Page 21. Sidney Poitier in A Raisin in the Sun (1959). Photo Source: Wikimedia Commons/ Friedman-Abeles.

Page 21. Billy Dee Williams in A Taste of Honey on Broadway (1960). Photo source: Wikimedia Commons/Bill Doll and Company.

Page 21. Ruby Dee and Jackie Robinson. Photo source: From the New York Public Library.

Page 23. Ruby Dee (1972). Photo source: Wikimedia Commons/Chicago Sun Times.

Page 23. Eartha Kitt as Catwoman (1967). Photo source: Wikimedia Commons/ABC Television.

Page 23. Cicely Tyson (1973). Photo source: Wikimedia Commons/Hans Peters.

Page 25. Misty Copeland in "Coppelia" (2014). Photo source: Wikimedia Commons/Naim Chidiac Abu Dhabi Festival.

Page 25. Alvin Ailey Dance Company Performing "Revelations" (2011). Photo source: Wikimedia Commons/Knight Foundation.

Page 29. Toni Morrison (1970). Photo source: Wikimedia Commons/"The Bluest Eye."

Page 29. James Baldwin (1974). Photo source: Wikimedia Commons/Rob Croes.

Page 29. Zora Neale Hurston Beating the Hountar Drum (1937). Photo source: Wikimedia Commons/World Telegram Staff Photographer.

Page 29. Langston Hughes Rehearsing New Play in Chicago, IL (1942). Photo source: Library of Congress/Jack Delano.

Page 31. Octavia Butler (2005). Photo source: Wikimedia Commons/Nikolas Coukouma.

Page 33. Newsboy Carrying the Chicago Defender (1942). Photo source: Library of Congress/Jack Delano.

Page 33. Cover of *The Crisis*'s October 1914 issue, which was dedicated to children's issues. Photo source: The New York Public Library.

Page 33. Cover of *The Crisis*. Photo source: From the New York Public Library.

Page 34. John B. Russwurm, Co-publisher, Freedom's Journal. Photo source: Blackpast.com/Public Domain Image.

Page 34. Samuel E. Cornish, Co-publisher, Freedom's Journal. Photo source: Blackpast.com/Public Domain Image.

Page 37. Founded in 1945, Ebony was the first Black-oriented magazine in the United States to attain national circulation. (Britannica.com). Photo courtesy of Kimberly Singleton.

Page 37. Tyra Banks at the 2012 Time 100 Gala. Photo source: Wikimedia Commons/David Shankbone.

Page 38. Matthew Henson Immediately after the Sledge Journey to the North Pole in 1909. Photo source: Wikimedia Commons/Photographer unknown.

Page 40. Bessie Coleman and Her Plane (1922). Photo source: Wikimedia Commons/Photographer unknown.

Page 42. Neil deGrasse Tyson (2012). Photo source: Wikimedia Commons/Genevieve.

Page 45. Frederick McKinley Jones Standing Next to a Truck Outfitted with a Mobile Refrigeration Unit, c. 1950. Photo Source: The Minnesota Historical Society.

Page 45. Dr. Patricia E. Bath (1984). Photo source: Wikimedia Commons/UCLA Jules Stein Eye Institute.

Page 47. Venus Williams (2013), US Open. Photo source: Wikimedia Commons/Ewin Martinez.

Page 47. Serena Williams (2013), US Open. Photo source: Wikimedia Commons/Edwin Martinez.

Page 49. Tommie Smith (Gold Medalist/200m), John Carlos (Bronze Medalist/200m) at the 1968 Olympics in Mexico City. Photo source: Wikimedia Commons/Angelo Cozzi (Mondadori Publishers).

Page 51. Football Team Kneeling in Prayer. Photo source: phhere.com / CCO Public Domain.

Page 52. Graves Hall, Morehouse College 2016. Photo source: Thomson200, Creative Commons CC0 1.0 Universal Public Domain Dedication.

Page 53. Fisk University, Nashville, Tennessee by Eula. Own work, CC By 3.0, Wikimedia Commons.

Page 53. Young Hall, Lincoln University of Missouri. Photo source: Wikimedia Commons/ TheCatalyst31.

Page 56. Kimberly Singleton at Howard University. Photo courtesy of Kimberly Singleton.

Page 61. Alpha Phi Alpha Fraternity Fourth Annual Conference in Ann Arbor, Michigan (1911). Photo source: Wikimedia Commons.

Page 61. Kappa Alpha Psi Chapter at Wilberforce University (Ohio) in 1922. Photo credit: Wikimedia Commons/Wilberforce University. Public Domain.

Page 63. Rho Chapter of Alpha Kappa Alpha Sorority in 1921, Berkeley, California. Photo source: Blackpast.org.

Page 63. Alpha Kappa Alpha Sorority NYPL in 1922. Photo Source: From The New York Public Library.

Page 65. Tuskegee Airmen 332nd Fighter Group Pilots (1945). Photo source: Wikimedia Commons/Toni Frissell.

Page 69. African American Family Going to Church in Chicago, IL, 1941. Photo source: Library of Congress/Edwin Rosskam.

Page 70. Martin Luther King Jr. Speaking at the University of Pittsburgh (1966). Photo source: Wikimedia Commons/The Owl.

Page 73. Judge Ketanji Brown Jackson. Photo source: Wikimedia Commons/Wikicago [Creative Commons Attribution-Share Alike 4.0 International license].

Page 75. Fannie Lou Hamer at the Democratic National Convention in Atlantic City, NJ (1964). Photo source: Wikimedia Commons/World Report Magazine, Warren Leffler, restored by Adam Cuerden.

Page 75. Thurgood Marshall. Photo source: Wikimedia Commons/Library of Congress. Public Domain digital ID cph.3b07878.

Page 75. Malcolm X Waiting for a Press Conference to Begin on March 26, 1964. Photo source: Wikimedia Commons/Marion S. Trikosko. Public Domain.

Page 77. Daisy Bates (1935). Photo source: Wikimedia Commons/Bernard Botturi.

Page 77. Kamala Harris Being Sworn In as Vice President of the United States (2021). Photo source: Wikimedia Commons/The White House.

Page 77. Representative John Lewis. Photo source: Wikimedia Commons/United States House of Representatives.

Page 77. Shirley Chisolm speaking. Photo Source: From the New York Public Library/ CCO 1.0 Dedication

Page 81. Black Lives Matter March (2020). Photo source: Wikimedia Commons/Taymaz Valley.

Page 81. Howard University's Trayvon Martin Million Hoodies Rally in Washington, DC (2012). Photo source: Wikimedia Commons/Elvert Barnes.

Page 82. Colored Waiting Room (1940). Photo source: Wikimedia Commons/Jack Delano.
Page 83. Drinking fountain on the county courthouse lawn, Halifax, North Carolina. 1938. Photo Source: From the New York Public Library.